Code It
Yourself

CODING
GAMES FROM SCRATCH

An Augmented Reading Experience

By Rachel Ziter

CAPSTONE PRESS
a capstone imprint

Download the Capstone app!

- Ask an adult to download the Capstone 4D app.
- Scan the cover and stars inside the book for additional content.

When you scan a spread, you'll find
fun extra stuff to go with this book!
You can also find these things
on the web at www.capstone4D.com
using the password: coding.games

Dabble Lab is published by Capstone Press
1710 Roe Crest Drive
North Mankato, Minnesota 56003
www.mycapstone.com

Library of Congress Cataloging-in-Publication Data
Names: Ziter, Rachel, author.
Title: Coding games from Scratch : 4D an augmented reading experience / by Rachel Ziter.
Description: North Mankato, Minnesota : Capstone Press, [2019] | Series: Dabble lab. Code it yourself 4D | Includes bibliographical
    references and index. | Audience: Ages 8-10.
Identifiers: LCCN 2018010607 (print) | LCCN 2018014353 (ebook) | ISBN 9781515766612 (eBook PDF) |
    ISBN 9781515766582 (hardcover) | ISBN 9781543536119 (pbk.)
Subjects: LCSH: Scratch (Computer program language)—Juvenile literature. | Computer games—Programming—Juvenile literature. |
    Computer programming—Juvenile literature. | Microcomputers—Programming—Juvenile literature.
Classification: LCC QA76.73.S345 (ebook) | LCC QA76.73.S345 Z58 2019 (print) | DDC 794.8/1525–dc23
LC record available at https://lccn.loc.gov/2018010607

Designer: Heidi Thompson

Photo Credits
Shutterstock: AlexZaitsev, Cover, Kotkoa, Cover, Phil's Mommy, 6
"Scratch is a trademark of Massachusetts Institute of Technology, which does not sponsor, endorse, or authorize this content.
See scratch.mit.edu for more information."

Printed and bound in the United States of America.
PA017

Table of Contents

What Is Coding?

Playing with an app on your smartphone. Clicking through a website. Without even realizing it, you're using coding. Coding is the language used to communicate with a computer. By creating a set of code, you're writing directions in a language that the computer can follow. Although computers may seem super smart, that's not the case! The only reason computers know how to do anything is because they have been coded to do it. A computer's code—the very specific directions given by a person—allows it to be the super-smart device we all know and love. The reality is, anyone can learn to code. In this book we'll be creating projects using one coding language in particular: Scratch.

What Is Scratch?

Scratch is an online coding platform that uses colorful coding blocks to create everything from games to presentations to animation. The colored blocks are sorted into categories like **Motion**, **Looks**, and **Sound**. By connecting the colorful blocks, you can start coding whatever comes to mind. For example, if you want to code a character to move around and make noise, you would start with an **Events** block, then add a **Motion** block, and finish with a **Sound** block. (You can also use a Control block to make the events repeat as many times as you'd like.)

Scratch runs on Adobe Flash Player, so make sure your software is up-to-date. To download and install Flash, go to: https://get.adobe.com/flashplayer/

TIP:

The projects in this book build in difficulty. If you've never coded before, start with the first project and work your way through. If something doesn't make sense in a later project, try going back to earlier projects to find the answer.

Creating a Scratch Account

To create the projects in this book, you will need a Scratch account. To get started, go to: www.scratch.mit.edu. In the upper right corner, click the *Join Scratch* button.

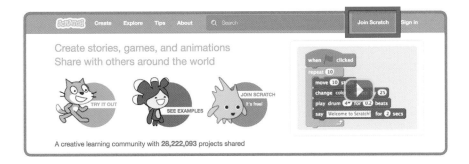

A window will pop up and ask you to create a Scratch username and password. Pick a password you can remember.

The next window will ask for your birth month/year. This is just to make sure you are old enough to use Scratch. If you are younger than 12, you'll need a parent's email to get permission.

The next window will ask for an email address. Scratch will send one email—to confirm your email address—when you sign up. After that, you'll only get emails if you need to reset your password.

Enter your email address and we will send you an email to confirm your account.

Email address

Confirm email address

☐ Receive updates from the Scratch Team

How to Use Scratch

Once you've created your Scratch account, you will see your username in the top right corner of the Scratch homepage. If you don't see your username, you need to sign in. Click *sign in* and enter the username and password that you've created.

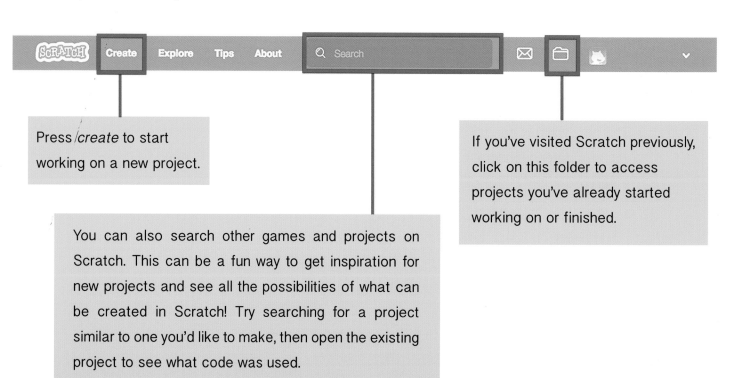

Press *create* to start working on a new project.

If you've visited Scratch previously, click on this folder to access projects you've already started working on or finished.

You can also search other games and projects on Scratch. This can be a fun way to get inspiration for new projects and see all the possibilities of what can be created in Scratch! Try searching for a project similar to one you'd like to make, then open the existing project to see what code was used.

When you click *create*, your screen will look like this:

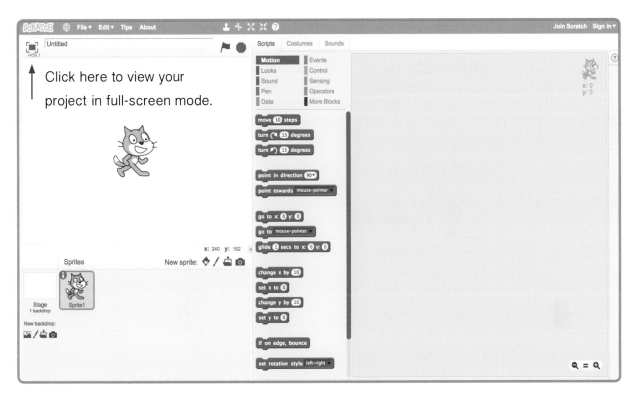

Click here to view your project in full-screen mode.

TOOLS

These tools are found at the top of the screen. They are helpful for creating new projects. Click on the tool you want to use—it will turn blue and the mouse will turn into the tool. Then click on the item you'd like to duplicate, cut, grow, or shrink.

stamp—The stamp is used to duplicate anything in your project. To use this tool, click on the icon so the cursor turns into the stamp, then click whatever you'd like to copy. You can click on a premade character or even a set of code.

scissors—The scissors are used to delete items in your project.

outward arrows—The arrows facing outward are used to grow characters. Continue clicking on the character until it is the desired size.

inward arrows—The arrows facing inward are used to shrink characters. Continue clicking on the character until it is the desired size.

WHAT IS A SPRITE?

A sprite is any moveable character or object used in a project. Sprites can be selected through the Scratch Library, created using drawing tools, or uploaded from the computer. Scratch Cat is an example of a sprite!

All sprites can be accessed in this box:

Sprite Library

NAME YOUR PROJECT HERE

This screen shows you what your project will look like when it's finished. In this area you can arrange your sprites on top of your background however you'd like for your project.

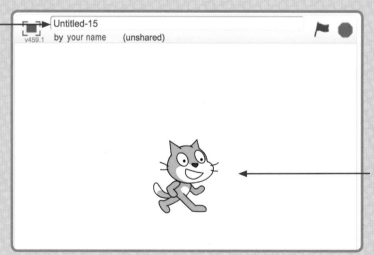

Untitled-15

v459.1   by your name   (unshared)

Scratch Cat will automatically appear on every project you start. He is the face of Scratch. If you don't want to use him in your project, it's OK! You can select whichever sprite you would like. But Scratch Cat will always appear with a new project to get you started.

alien head—Click to open the Sprite Library and select a sprite. All sprites are sorted alphabetically. You can choose anything from a dinosaur sprite to cheesy puffs to an airplane.

 paintbrush—Click on the paintbrush to open the paint tools and create your own sprite.

 folder—Click on the folder to upload an image from your computer to use as a sprite.

 camera—Click on the camera to use a picture from your computer as a sprite. A box will pop up asking to access the camera. Press *allow* to let Scratch access your computer's camera.

NAME YOUR SPRITE HERE

Click the blue ⓘ to open the sprite's information.

If a sprite is flipping upside down, change its rotation style here.

When you have selected a sprite, you will see three tabs in the top right corner: **Scripts**, **Costumes**, and **Sounds**.

Code blocks are color coded. To figure out which category a certain block is in, look at the color of the block and match it with the category.

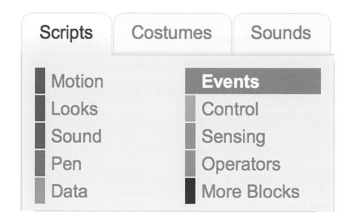

SCRIPTS TAB:

The Scripts tab is where you will create the code for all your projects. When you click on the Scripts tab, you will have access to the different code blocks needed to create projects.

Motion: These blocks are used to create movement. Using these blocks, you can tell your sprite to move around the screen, go to a particular place, turn, and more.

Looks: Here you will find the code needed to make your sprite or project change colors, grow, shrink, swap backgrounds, switch costumes, and much more! You can even code your sprite to say or think certain things. (When you code it with a *say* block, a speech bubble will appear above the sprite. The *say* and *think* blocks are here rather than in **Sound** because your sprite won't actually make any noise with these two blocks.)

Sound: Turn up the volume! The blocks in this category add sound to your sprites and/or background.

Pen: These blocks allow your sprites to draw lines wherever they move. (For example, if your sprite moves, then turns 90 degrees four times, you can create a square.) The size, color, and shade of the pen can also be programmed here.

Data: Here you can create variables to use within a project. A variable is a value that can be changed throughout the course of a project. (For example, you can use a variable for the number of lives a sprite has in a game.)

Events: These are your start commands. All code has a start command. This tells the program when it needs to start. These blocks will be the first piece used in any code you write. The most commonly used start command in this book will be the green flag.

Control: These blocks control how long certain things happen and if one thing causes another to start. There are repeat loops, wait commands, cloning blocks, and *if then* statements called conditional statements. (For example, *if* a sprite touches a certain color, *then* it needs to react in a certain way.) The *if then* conditional block will be one of the most used in this book.

Sensing: These blocks are used to detect things—like touching a certain sprite or color—in your code. They are often paired with the *if then* conditional block from Control. (For example, "If touching color blue, then the sprite jumps three times.")

Operators: These code blocks are used to combine codes or set a random range for something within a set of code. They will always be combined with other code blocks when used.

More Blocks: You won't see any blocks in this category at first—that's because you must create any blocks that go here. It can be helpful to create a block when you need to use a big piece of code repeatedly in a set of commands.

In Scratch, code blocks snap together like puzzle pieces. Simply drag the blocks together to make them attach. The code you create will run in whatever order you place the blocks. To take the blocks apart, pull from the bottom and down. If you remove a single piece, all the blocks attached below will stay connected to that piece. (You must pull each one off from the bottom.) To throw away a block you no longer want or need, drag it back to the category you originally selected it from and let go.

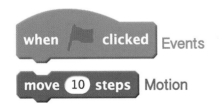

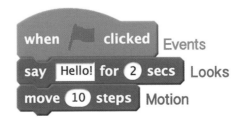

The code block on the right starts with the green flag being clicked. (This is the start command.) Next the sprite will say "Hello!" for two seconds. Once the two seconds have passed, the sprite will move 10 steps.

COSTUMES:

Here you can edit a sprite's appearance. You can also create your own sprite, or add a new costume to an existing sprite. Different costumes can be used to make it look like a sprite is moving. (Some sprites—like Scratch Cat—automatically come with more than one costume.) Multiple costumes are key to making your sprite look animated. Keep in mind that while you may have multiple costumes, there is still only one sprite!

You can name your costumes here.

When you open the Costumes tab, you will see tools you can use to customize your sprite.

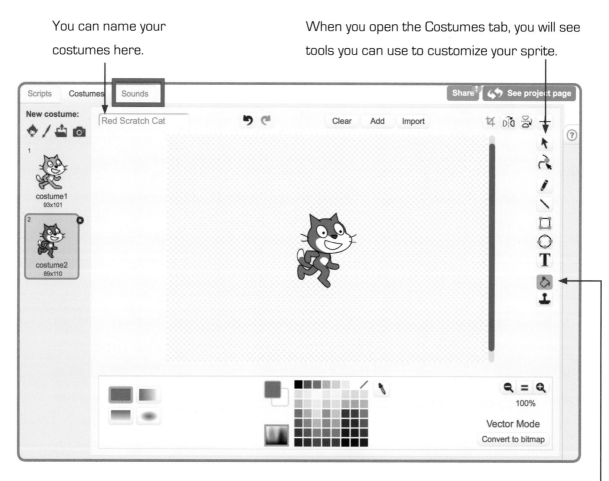

For this costume we used the paint bucket to make Scratch Cat red instead of his usual orange.

SOUNDS:

Once you've started a project, you can add sounds to your creation. To add a sound to a project, first select the sound from the library. You will later add it into the project through coding.

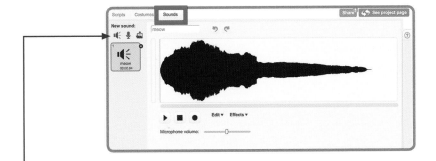

Each sprite comes with its own sound. Scratch Cat's sound is *meow*. Other sprites usually come with simple sounds like *pop*. Sprites that are imported or created using the graphic design tools do not have any sounds attached. To add a sound from the library, click on the speaker button.

SOUND LIBRARY:

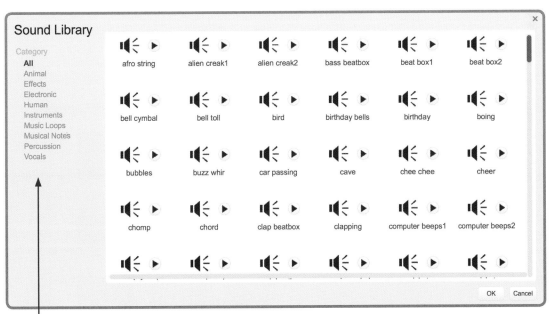

You can search for sounds easily by using the categories on the left side. The sounds within the library are sorted alphabetically to make them easier to find.

BACKDROPS:

Just like with sprites, there are lots of ways to access backdrops in Scratch and make them your own. You can select, create, upload, or snap a picture. The buttons used to create a new backdrop can be found on the bottom left corner of your screen, under the sprites section. There are four buttons you will use:

 mountain landscape—This icon opens the Backdrop Library so you can select a backdrop.

 paintbrush—This icon opens the paint tools, allowing you to create and name your own background.

 folder—This icon lets you upload an image from your computer to use as a background.

 camera—This icon lets you take a picture from your computer and use it as a background. (Note: When you click the camera, a pop-up box will ask to access the camera. Press *allow* to use the camera to create a backdrop.)

Backdrops are sorted by category and alphabetically in the Backdrop Library.

HOW TO PLAY

Move your car sprites until one of them reaches the colored finish line at the end. You'll also learn how to edit your sprites' color and create your own background.

LET'S GET STARTED!

STEP 1: Log in to Scratch and click *create* to start a new project. Then select the scissors tool at the top of the screen and click on Scratch Cat to delete him. (You'll use a different sprite for this game.) Next click the alien head icon. This will open the Sprite Library. Click on the transportation category and select a car.

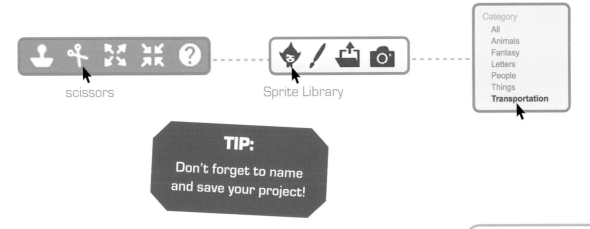

scissors

Sprite Library

Category
All
Animals
Fantasy
Letters
People
Things
Transportation

TIP:
Don't forget to name and save your project!

STEP 2: Click on the paintbrush icon under *New backdrop* to create your race backdrop. Name it *race* in the upper left-hand corner (on the opposite side of the screen).

OPTION: You can change the color of your race car using the paint bucket icon on the Costumes tab. Select the color you want from the color grid at the bottom of the page.

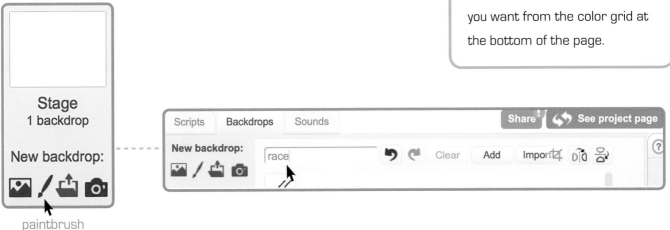

Stage
1 backdrop

New backdrop:

paintbrush

Scripts   Backdrops   Sounds

Share   See project page

New backdrop: race   Clear   Add   Import

STEP 3: Use the drawing tools to create a race track with three lanes. When finished, it should look like this:

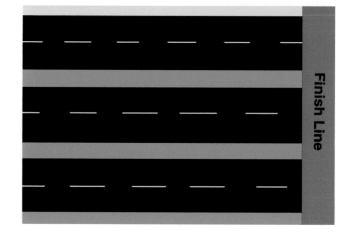

First use the paint bucket to fill in the background with green.

Use the rectangle tool to draw three lanes on your road. Choose the black filled-in option at the bottom.

Use the line tool to add one yellow line down the middle of each lane. Hold shift to make the line straight. (You can change the width so the line is thicker.)

Select a black line and change the width so it is thicker than the yellow line. Hold down shift to draw black lines through each of the yellow lines, creating the dashes on the road.

Use the rectangle tool to create a red finish line at the end of the race. (Select the filled-in option and add it to the screen vertically, in the opposite direction of your lanes.)

Use the text tool to type *Finish Line* and add the text box to your rectangle at the end. (Make sure your font is a different color than your finish line.) You will need to rotate the text box at the top so it sits vertically on top of the finish line.

Use this dot to rotate.

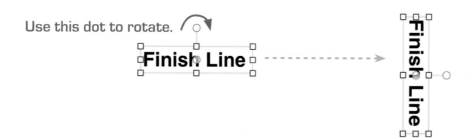

Last, but not least, use the paint bucket to make the sky above your race track blue.

STEP 4: Now that your car sprite and race track are created, you can start adding code. Click on the car sprite, then add the code shown here to its Scripts tab.

This code will be activated with the green flag.

This block causes the cars to start with an X coordinate of -200, making the cars start on the left of the screen.

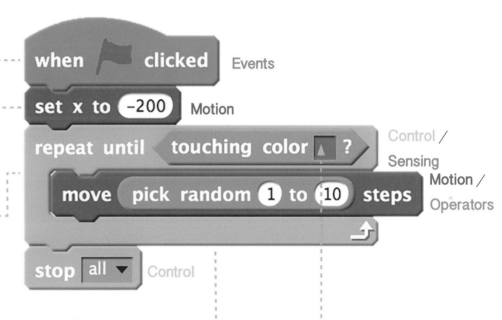

Add a *repeat until* loop. The motion inside of the loop will continue until the sprite has touched the color red—the finish line!

The combination of these two blocks will cause your sprite to move at a random speed, which is needed in any race.

When the color red is touched, the sprite will stop moving and the race will end.

TOUCHING COLOR

To select the desired code for the color-sensing block, click inside the square. A small white finger cursor will appear. When the finger cursor appears, move the cursor to the color you'd like to select and click on it. The color you selected should now fill the square in the color-sensing block.

STEP 5: Duplicate your car sprite twice using the stamp tool at the top of the screen. At the end of this step, you should have two exact copies of your sprite, along with the code that you programmed onto it.

 Find this tool at the top of the page. Click your car sprite twice to duplicate two times. You should now have a total of three sprites.

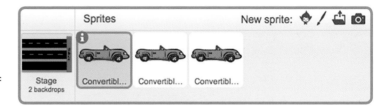

STEP 6: Go to the Costumes tab for the two new sprites you created and change their colors so they're no longer identical. (You want three separate cars so you can see which one wins the race!)

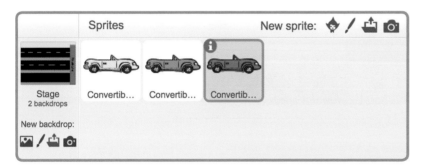

 Fill in your sprites using the paint bucket so all the cars look different.

TIP:

Use the zoom symbol to get closer to the sprite. This will make it easier to fill in small areas, like the door handle.

🔍 = 🔍

STEP 7: Arrange the sprites on the background to the left of your screen. Then click the green flag to play and see which car wins!

TIP:

Click on the blue square in the upper left corner of your screen to see your finished game in full-screen mode.

Use this link to see the finished game and watch the cars race toward the finish line:

https://scratch.mit.edu/projects/174138379/

Monkey Jumping on the Bed!

HOW TO PLAY

For this game you'll be working with the animal kingdom! Create and code a monkey sprite to move around randomly until he is caught. If he's caught, the backdrop will switch to a *game over* screen.

LET'S GET STARTED!

STEP 1: Click *create* to start a new project, then select the scissors at the top of the screen and click on Scratch Cat to delete him. Next click the alien head icon in the sprite panel and select the monkey from the Sprite Library. (You can narrow it down using the *Animals* category.)

scissors   Sprite Library

STEP 2: In your backdrop panel, click on the mountain landscape icon and choose the bedroom background. This will automatically be saved as *bedroom1*.

landscape

STEP 3: Go to your backdrop tools and use the paintbrush to create a new backdrop. (This will be your *game over* screen.)

paintbrush

winner   Name this backdrop *winner*.

Use the paint bucket tool and, on the bottom right, select two colors to fill in the background with the dual-color effects. (Click on your blank backdrop to fill it with color.)

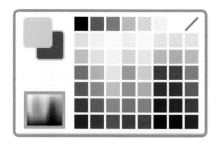

Use the text icon and select the color black to type the winner message. Write whatever you want to appear at the end of your game. Use the sizing dots around the text to make it as large as you'd like.

You Caught Me!

STEP 4: Time to add sound! Select your monkey sprite. Then go to the Sounds tab.

Click on the speaker icon to open the Sound Library and select the *rattle* sound effect. (Remember, sounds are sorted alphabetically to make it easier to find them.)

rattle

rattle   rooster   scratch beatbox

Use this dark gray bar to slide up and down through the different sounds. To preview the sound, click on the *play* button next to it. Click *OK* on the bottom right to select it.

Once your sound is selected, it should show under the Sounds tab, along with *pop*—the sound that automatically comes with most sprites. If the *rattle* sound isn't there, go back into the Sound Library and re-select it.

1
pop
00:00.02

2
rattle
00:00.59

Note: Just because you select a sound on one sprite doesn't mean it automatically shows up on another sprite in your projects. Sounds must be selected for each sprite that needs noise.

STEP 5: Under the Scripts tab, add this code to your monkey sprite.

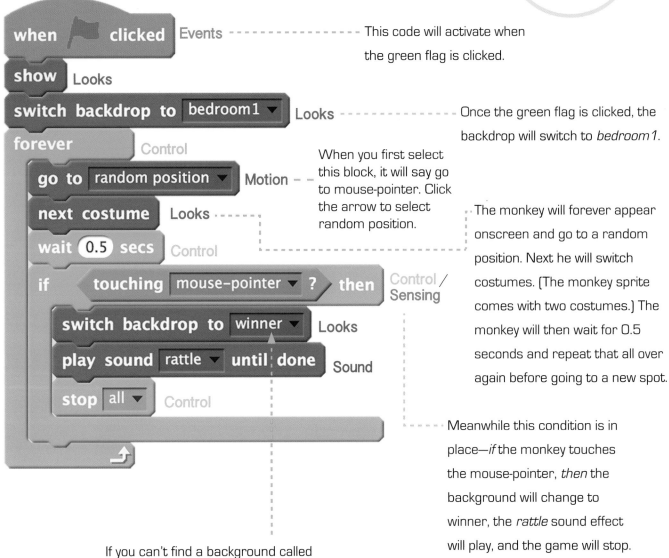

when [flag] clicked — Events ---------------- This code will activate when the green flag is clicked.

show — Looks

switch backdrop to bedroom1 ▼ — Looks ---------- Once the green flag is clicked, the backdrop will switch to *bedroom1*.

forever — Control

go to random position ▼ — Motion -- When you first select this block, it will say go to mouse-pointer. Click the arrow to select random position.

next costume — Looks -----

wait 0.5 secs — Control

if touching mouse-pointer ▼ ? then — Control / Sensing

switch backdrop to winner ▼ — Looks

play sound rattle ▼ until done — Sound

stop all ▼ — Control

The monkey will forever appear onscreen and go to a random position. Next he will switch costumes. (The monkey sprite comes with two costumes.) The monkey will then wait for 0.5 seconds and repeat that all over again before going to a new spot.

Meanwhile this condition is in place—*if* the monkey touches the mouse-pointer, *then* the background will change to winner, the *rattle* sound effect will play, and the game will stop.

If you can't find a background called *winner*, go back to your backdrops tab and be sure that you named it correctly.

You're finished! Click on *See project page* to play your game

and try to catch the monkey. See the finished game here: https://scratch.mit.edu/projects/154122791/

HOW TO PLAY

Code Scratch Cat to fall from a random spot in the sky in hopes that a bat will catch him and carry him to safety. If Scratch Cat falls without the bat catching him, the game is over. If the bat catches Scratch Cat and brings him to the safe button, he is saved!

LET'S GET STARTED!

STEP 1: Start a new project—don't forget to name it! Then click on the mountain icon to open the Backdrop Library. Select the *woods* backdrop.

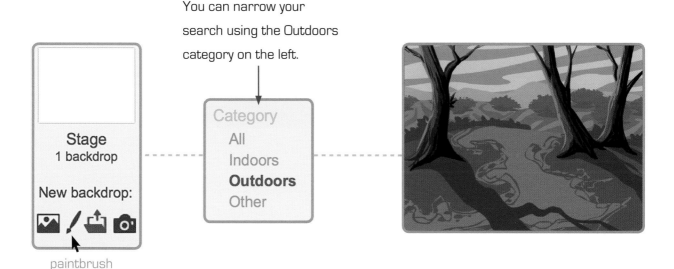

You can narrow your search using the Outdoors category on the left.

paintbrush

Once you have selected the correct backdrop, go to the Backdrops tab and add a small, filled-in rectangle to the bottom of your screen. Make this rectangle pink. (Once you get the hang of coding, feel free to use any color not in the background or on any of your sprites. The sprite colors are orange, black, and brown.)

Make sure to choose the filled-in rectangle icon!

STEP 2: Use the paintbrush to create two new backdrops. You'll need a *winner* backdrop and a *game over* backdrop.

New backdrop:

paintbrush

Name both backdrops in the box at the top left.

winner

game over

Use the paint bucket to fill in both backdrops with your desired color(s).

Use the text tool to type your winning and losing messages on the correct backdrops.

Scratch Cat is Saved!

GAME OVER

Feel free to add extras to the screens if you'd like!

STEP 3: Leave Scratch Cat on the project; you will be using him as a sprite. Open the Sprite Library and select a bat sprite and a button sprite. (You can find these in the *Animals* and *Things* categories.) You should now have three sprites. In the button sprite's information section, name it *safe button*.

Sprite Library

Note: If you'd like to save a sprite other than Scratch Cat in this game, now is the time to make the switch. All code placed on Scratch Cat in these directions will need to go on the new sprite you've selected if you wait till the end!

STEP 4: Click on the button sprite, then open the Costumes tab to customize it. Use the text tool to add the word *safe* to the button sprite. Feel free to change the button's color using the paint bucket. Once you're finished, drag it to the safe spot of your choice in your game!

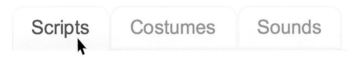

STEP 5: Click on the Scripts tab and add the below code to the button sprite. Remember to match the code blocks to the correct category using their color.

Events - - - - - - This code tells the button sprite to show up when the green flag is clicked, and hide whenever the background switches to *winner* or *game over*.

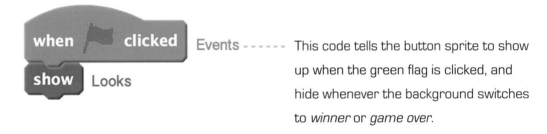

STEP 6: Select the bat sprite, and add the four code blocks you see below to its Scripts tab.

Scripts   Costumes   Sounds

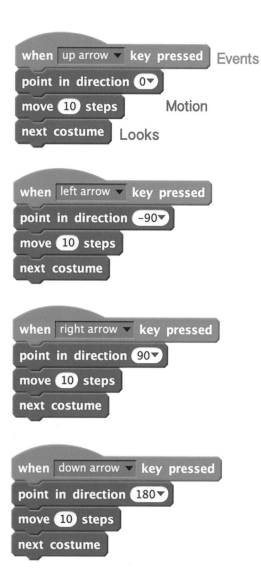

when up arrow key pressed   **Events**
point in direction 0
move 10 steps   **Motion**
next costume   **Looks**

when left arrow key pressed
point in direction -90
move 10 steps
next costume

when right arrow key pressed
point in direction 90
move 10 steps
next costume

when down arrow key pressed
point in direction 180
move 10 steps
next costume

These code blocks will activate when one of the arrow keys is pressed. The bat will then point in the appropriate direction, move, and switch costumes.

To select which arrow key will move the bat, find the below block in **Events**. It will say *space key* at first. Click the arrow to open the drop-down menu and select the correct key.

when space key pressed

To select which direction the bat will move, find the below block in **Motion**. (The drop-down menu will help you understand which number represents which direction.)

point in direction 90

The costume block is used to make the bat look like it's flapping its wings. It will change between these two costumes as it moves. (Both costumes come with the bat sprite.)

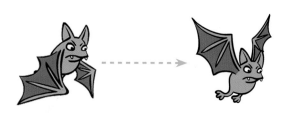

STEP 7: Finish the bat by adding these last few blocks of code to its Scripts tab.

```
when [flag] clicked   Events
show   Looks
set x to 0
```

```
when backdrop switches to winner ▼
hide   Looks
```

```
when backdrop switches to game over ▼
hide   Looks
```

These codes make the bat appear when the green flag is clicked, then set its X coordinate to 0 (the center of the screen) at the start of the game, and hide on the *winner* and *game over* screens.

```
when space ▼ key pressed
```

Use the drop-down menu to select the option you need.

Imagine your Scratch work space is a big coordinate plane.

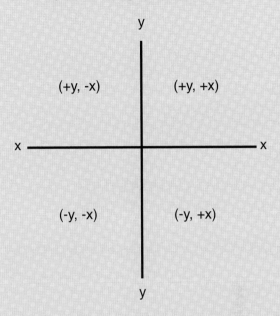

Changing the X and Y in the **Motion** block refers to the X and Y axis of a coordinate plane. If you have a positive Y coordinate, it will be found on the upper half of the plane. If you have a negative Y coordinate, it will be found on the lower half. If you have a positive X coordinate, it will be found on the right side. If you have a negative X coordinate, it will be found on the left side.

A **quadrant** is any of the four quarters into which something is divided by two real or imaginary lines (in this case, the X and Y axes) that intersect each other at right angles.

As you move your mouse around the plane, the X and Y coordinates on the bottom will change to show the mouse coordinates. X:0 Y:0 indicates that you are in the middle of the screen or coordinate plane. This is called the **origin**.

STEP 8: Click on your Scratch Cat sprite and add this code to his Scripts tab.

when ⚑ clicked Events

show Looks

switch backdrop to woods ▼

set y to 180 Motion

set x to pick random -240 to 240 Motion / Operators

forever Control

   change y by -1 Motion

   if touching Bat1 ▼ ? then Control / Sensing

      go to Bat1 ▼ Motion

   if touching color ☐ ? then Control / Sensing

      switch backdrop to game over ▼ Looks

      hide

      stop all ▼ Control

   if touching safe button ▼ ? and touching Bat1 ▼ ? then Control / Operators / Sensing

      switch backdrop to winner ▼ Looks

      hide

      stop all ▼ Control

When the green flag is clicked, Scratch Cat will appear and the background will change to the woods backdrop.

Scratch Cat will set his Y coordinate to 180 so he starts at the top of the screen. (The Y coordinate is the position along the Y axis, which runs up and down. 180 is the highest Y position on the Scratch grid.)

Scratch Cat's X coordinate is set to random -240 to 240 so he falls from a different spot on the X axis each time the game is played. (The X coordinate is the position along the X axis, which runs left to right. -240 to 240 is the X coordinate range for the Scratch window.) The bottom section of code is held inside a forever loop. That means it will repeat continuously throughout the game. The Y coordinate will change by -1, causing Scratch Cat to fall downward. (To make him fall faster, change the number to a more negative number, like -2 or -3.)

There are three different conditions—*if thens*—that can happen to Scratch Cat. To code what happens if a condition is met, the code blocks go inside the loop of the *if then* block.

1. The **first condition** tells Scratch Cat that *if* he touches the bat, *then* he should move wherever the bat does. (This **Motion** block will originally say *go to mouse pointer*, select *bat1* in the drop-down bar.)
2. The **second condition** says that *if* Scratch Cat touches the pink rectangle at the bottom of the screen, *then* the screen will switch to game over, Scratch Cat will hide, and everything will stop.
3. The **final condition** says that *if* the bat reaches the safe button with Scratch Cat, *then* the background will switch to the *winner* backdrop and stop all. (To select both the safe button and the bat, you will need to select the *and* block from Operators and both sprite blocks from Sensing. Try building this block separately before dropping it into your Control block.)

TIP:
See page 17 for a reminder on how to select the correct color in your Sensing block.

Use this link to check out the finished game and try your luck at saving Scratch Cat: https://scratch.mit.edu/projects/158576405/

How Did the Crab Cross the Road?

HOW TO PLAY

Use the arrow keys to move your crab across a busy street without getting hit by a car. If the crab is hit, you'll be sent back to the beginning. If the crab makes it safely across the street, you win!

LET'S GET STARTED!

STEP 1: Start a new project. Use the scissors to delete Scratch Cat, then open the Sprite Library. Select the crab sprite and a car sprite.

scissors   Sprite Library

STEP 2: Click on the paintbrush icon in the backdrop tools to draw your own road background that looks like what you see here:

New backdrop:

paintbrush

Use the filled-in rectangle to make the lanes.

Use the line tool to make the lines on your road.

*For more specific instructions on creating your road, check out step 3 in Race Game!

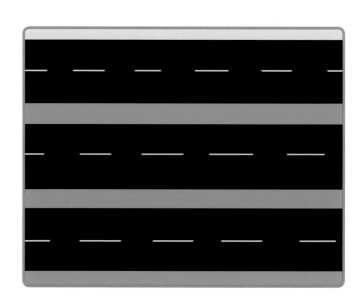

STEP 3: Add the code blocks you see below to your crab sprite.

These **Motion** and **Events** blocks control which direction the crab moves and by how much.

when up arrow ▼ key pressed Events
change y by 10 Motion

when left arrow ▼ key pressed
change x by −10

when right arrow ▼ key pressed
change x by 10

when space ▼ key pressed
change y by −10

STEP 4: Add the following code to the car sprite. This will create a screen scrolling effect in your game.

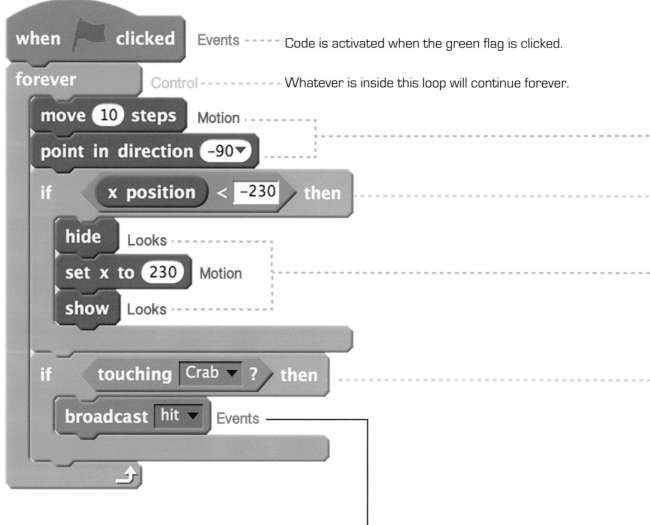

when 🏁 clicked   Events - - - - - Code is activated when the green flag is clicked.

forever   Control - - - - - - - - - Whatever is inside this loop will continue forever.

move (10) steps   Motion - - - - - - - -

point in direction (-90▼)

if (x position < -230) then

hide   Looks - - - - - - -

set x to (230)   Motion - - - - - - - - -

show   Looks - - - - - - - -

if (touching Crab ▼ ?) then

broadcast hit ▼   Events

Use the drop-down menu to select *new message*. Then create a new broadcast and name it *hit*.

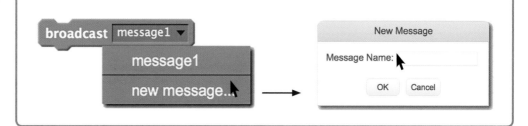

broadcast message1 ▼

message1

new message...

New Message

Message Name:

OK   Cancel

These two blocks will make the car move at a certain speed and to the left. That is the direction the screen scrolling code is also going. [Use a number larger than five in the first block to make the car go faster.]

Combine the inequality block from Operators and the X-position block from **Motion** to create this block. [Try combining them separately and then dragging them into your Control block.]

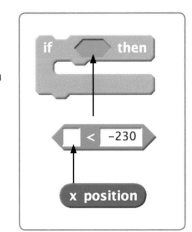

The combination of blocks inside the *if then* conditional statement will keep the car moving until the condition—*X position < -230*—has been met. [Note: -230 is the edge of the X axis. If the car kept moving beyond that, we wouldn't be able to see it!] If the car reaches an X coordinate less then -230, the sequence of code inside the loop will start. If the car reaches -230, we need it to hide, reposition itself onto the other side of the screen, and reappear. This creates the illusion of the car scrolling through the screen.

This conditional statement is activated when the car sprite touches the crab sprite. Whenever this happens you broadcast—send a message—to the crab telling it that it has been hit. [We will code what happens to the crab in another step.]

STEP 5: Change the rotation style of the car sprite so it doesn't flip upside down when it moves. To do this, click on the small letter ⓘ to open the sprite's information. Then click the side-to-side arrow in rotation style.

STEP 6: Once you have changed the rotation style, use the stamp tool to duplicate the car sprite twice. (You should now have a total of three cars.) In the Costumes tab, use the paint bucket to change the cars' colors so they don't all look the same. (Go back to Race Game if you need help.)

STEP 7: Add the below code to your crab sprite. This tells the crab to react to the *hit* message it will receive when the car touches it. (Use the drop-down menu in the Events block to select the correct option.)

STEP 8: Arrange the sprites on the screen as shown on the next page. (You may need to use the shrink tool to fit the sprites on the screen.)

shrink tool

To use the shrink tool, click on the inward-arrows icon, then continue clicking the sprite you'd like to shrink until it's the correct size.

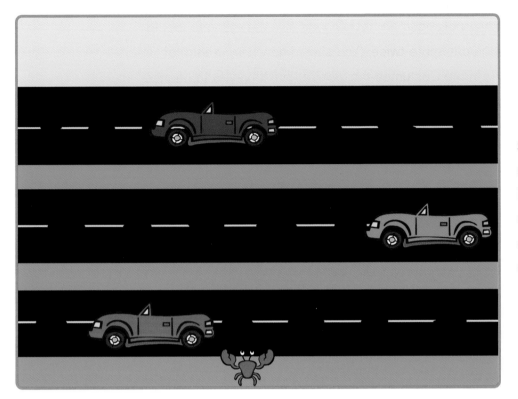

Stagger the car sprites along the lanes on the road so they move across the screen at different times.

To change the car speeds, edit the **Motion** block in the code.

move 10 steps

TIP:
You do not need to change the numbers on the **Motion** block when you drag it out from the selection area. The coordinates will update when you move the sprite. (It's okay if exact location of your crab is different from what you see here. Yours may be placed at a different location than the one shown.)

 **See project page** Click on *See project page* to play. Use the arrow keys to move your crab across the road. Don't get hit! Use this link to check out the finished game: https://scratch.mit.edu/projects/174141026/

Space Muffins

HOW TO PLAY

Use the up and down arrows to control a spaceship that is trying to destroy invading dinosaurs. To destroy the dinosaurs, click the space bar to blast muffins at them!

LET'S GET STARTED!

STEP 1: Open a new project and use the scissors to delete Scratch Cat. (Don't forget to name your project!) Then choose a spaceship, a muffin, and a dinosaur sprite from the Sprite Library.

scissors   Sprite Library

STEP 2: Use the paintbrush in your backdrop toolbar to create a new backdrop.

paintbrush

space

Name your new backdrop *space*.

Use the paint bucket to color the background black. Then use the paintbrush to add white stars. (You'll need to increase the paintbrush's thickness.)

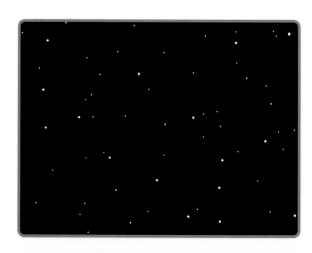

STEP 3: In the spaceships' Costumes tab, delete the *spaceship-b* costume by clicking the *x* in the upper right corner. Then duplicate the *spaceship-a* costume by clicking on the stamp tool at the top of your screen, then on the *spaceship-a* costume.

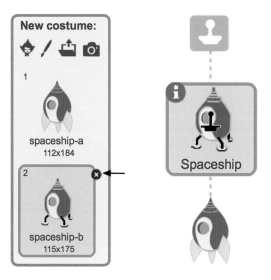

Change the first costume's name to *spaceship*. Then convert the second costume to bitmap mode by clicking *Convert to bitmap* at the bottom right of the screen. Use the grabber tool in the toolbar on the left to pull apart pieces of the ship. (You need to draw a box around each part of the spaceship you want to break apart and then drag it.) Name the second costume *crash*.

grabber tool

BITMAP MODE VS. VECTOR MODE

There are two different drawing modes in Scratch: **bitmap** and **vector**. Bitmap mode makes it easy to fill in backgrounds and shapes and is good for simple uses. However, in bitmap mode, you won't be able to resize or reshape anything you make. The drawing tools in vector mode are similar to tools in bitmap mode. However, in vector mode you can create another shape and still go back to a previous one and move it. In this mode, you can also reshape objects that you have made.

STEP 4: Arrange the spaceship sprite on the background as shown below.
Be sure to shrink the sprites to the right sizes using the shrink tool.
(The muffin should be about half the size of the spaceship.)

shrink tool

To rotate the spaceship, click on the ℹ to open the sprite's information. Turn the line on the direction circle until the ship is facing to the right.

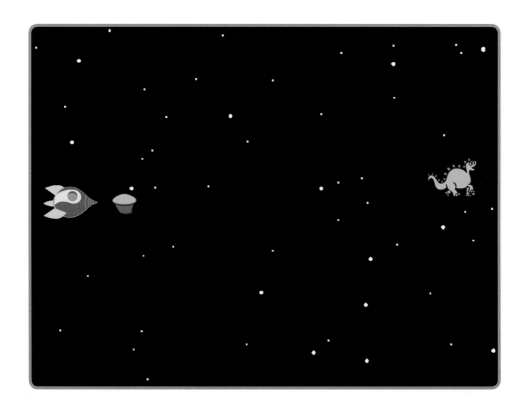

STEP 5: Go to the Sounds tab for the spaceship sprite and open the Sound Library. Select the *cymbal crash* effect. Then add the below code to your spaceship sprite's Scripts tab.

crash cymbal

This will tell the spaceship to move up or down with the arrow keys.

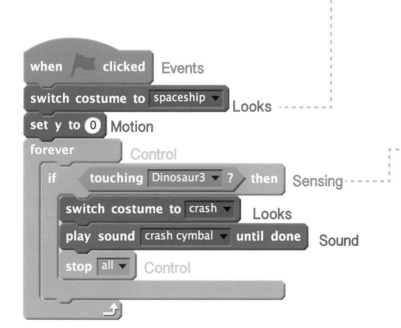

This block tells the spaceship that when the green flag is clicked, the spaceship's costume will switch to the intact spaceship. Then the ship will start in the middle of the Y axis (0).

There is one condition on the spaceship, saved within the forever loop. If the spaceship touches the dinosaur, the ship's costume will change to *crash*, the *cymbal crash* sound will play, and the game will stop. (The *stop all* code stops other codes in the game, like the dinosaurs invading.)

WHAT IS THE CLONING CODE BLOCK?

Before we go further, let's talk about the cloning block. You'll need it for the muffin and dinosaur sprites. If you preview the game using the link at the end, you'll notice that multiple dinosaurs invade and multiple muffins are blasted out. But so far, we have only one dinosaur and one muffin.

So how do you get from here to there? That's where the cloning block comes in. A clone is a copy of an existing sprite. Using code, you can tell your sprite(s) when to make a clone and give specifics on what you need that clone to do. The cloning blocks can be found in the Control category.

These blocks will be used in the next few parts of code:

To make multiple clones, pair the *create clone* block from Control with a forever loop or a repeat loop (also in the Control category) to create the desired number of clones.

Click on your muffin sprite, then open the Sounds tab. Open the Sound Library and select *laser2*. Then add the code blocks below to the muffin sprite.

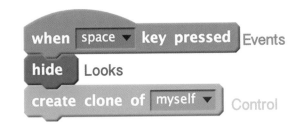

When the space bar is clicked, the original sprite will hide, and the muffin sprite will create a clone.

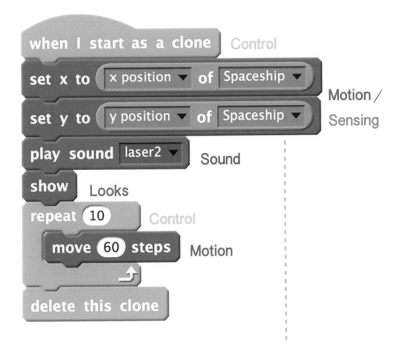

This code tells the muffin sprite that when it starts as a clone, its X and Y coordinates should be the same as those of the spaceship sprite. This will make it look like the muffin is blasting from the ship. Then the *laser2* sound will play, and the muffin will show, move across the screen, and disappear. (To make the muffin move faster or slower, increase or decrease the number in the *move __ steps* **Motion** block.)

Use the **Sensing** and **Motion** blocks to create the *set X to* and *set Y to* part of the spaceship code. Select the correct entry from the drop-down menu and drag it inside the *set X to* or *set Y to* code block. Then you can drag the complete block into place within your larger code block.

STEP 7: Add the below code blocks to the dinosaur sprite.

when ⚑ clicked   Events - - - - - - - - - - - - - - - - - This code starts when the green flag is clicked.

hide Looks

forever   Control - - - - - - - - - - - - - - - - - The original sprite will hide, and the dinosaur
 create clone of myself ▼   will create a clone every 1 – 7 seconds. (This will
 wait pick random ① to ⑦ secs   happen forever thanks to the forever loop.) The
   Operators   wait allows the dinosaurs to come out at random
    times throughout the game.

This code tells the cloned dinosaur sprites what to do when - - - - - - - - - - -
they are created. Once cloned, they must go to the far right of
the screen (X=240). Then their color will be set to something
random—this makes each dinosaur come out a different color.

when I start as a clone   Control · - - - - - - - - - -

set x to 240   Motion

set color ▼ effect to pick random ① to 200   Looks / Operators · - - - - -

set y to pick random –175 to 175   Motion / Operators · - - - - - - -

show Looks

point in direction –90▼   Motion · - - - - - - - - - -

repeat until ⟨ touching Muffin ▼ ? ⟩ or ⟨ x position < –200 ⟩   Control / Sensing /
            Operators / Motion · - - - - -
 change x by pick random –7 to –3   Motion / Operators

delete this clone   Control · - - - - - - - - - - - -

The clone must then set its Y coordinate to random location between -175 and 175. (This means the dinosaur will enter the screen at a random spot on the Y axis.) Then it will show and point to the left of the screen (-90). To create the *set Y to random* block, use the *set Y block* from **Motion** and the *pick random* block from Operators.

Then the dinosaur will change its X by a random number from -7 to -3. This controls how fast the dinosaur invades. The dinosaur will repeat this random change until it has touched the muffin or its X position is less than -200. (An X position of less than -200 means the dinosaur has passed the spaceship on the screen.) When either one of those things happen, the clone will delete.

Drag these blocks (Sensing, Operators, and **Motion**) together to make the big block. Then drag it inside the forever loop from the Control category.

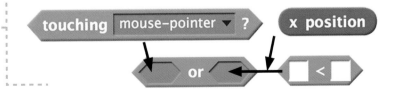

STEP 8: Click on your backdrop and open the Sounds tab. Select the *space ripple* sound. Then go to the Scripts tab and add this final code.

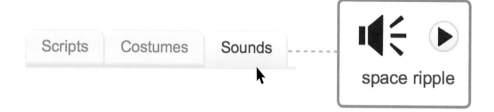

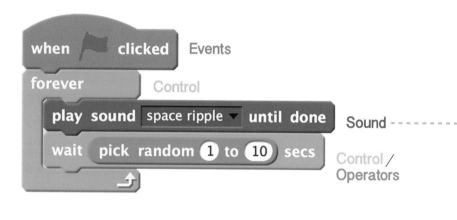

Sound - - - - - - - - - This code will play the *space ripple* sound at the start of the game and then at random times throughout the game. If you'd like the sound to play more often, make the range on the *pick random* block smaller.

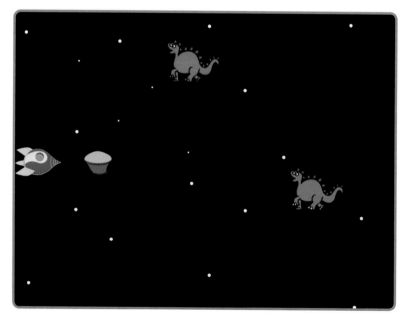

Click on the green flag to play your game. Use the arrow keys to move your spaceship and avoid the dinosaurs. Use the space bar to blast muffins at the dinosaurs before they destroy your ship! Use this link to see the finished game: https://scratch.mit.edu/projects/178325240/

Read More

Wainewright, Max. *Code Your Own Games!: 20 Games to Create with Scratch.* New York, NY. Sterling Children's Books, 2017.

Ziter, Rachel. *Coding in Scratch for Beginners: 4D An Augmented Reading Experience.* North Mankato, Minn.: Capstone Press, 2018.

Ziter, Rachel. *Making Music from Scratch: 4D An Augmented Reading Experience.* North Mankato, Minn.: Capstone Press, 2019.

Makerspace Tips

Download tips and tricks for using this book and others in a library makerspace.

Visit www.capstonepub.com/dabblelabresources

Internet Sites

Use Facthound to find Internet sites related to this book.

Visit www.facthound.com

Just type in 9781515766582 and go.

Coding Glossary

Bitmap mode: The drawing tools in this mode make it easy to fill in backgrounds and shapes. If you are making a quick shape or basic background, bitmap mode is a good choice. (Keep in mind that if you need to go back and resize a shape later, bitmap mode won't allow it.) To change between bitmap and vector mode, use the buttons on the bottom right of the design screen.

Broadcast: These code blocks can be found in the Events category of the Scripts tab. A broadcast is like sending a message.

Coding: Coding is the language used to communicate with a computer. By creating a set of code, you are writing directions in a language that the computer can follow. Code is very specific! Without code, computers wouldn't know how to do anything.

Conditional statement: A conditional statement is used in code when you need one thing to happen, but only if another does. (For example: If _____ happens, then _____ needs to happen.) These are also called *if then* statements.

Coordinate: A coordinate is an object's exact X-position and Y-position on a coordinate plane. Think of it as a very specific spot!

Coordinate plane: A coordinate plane is made up of an X and Y axis. These two axes run perpendicular to each other—one runs up and down, and the other runs right to left. When they meet, the axes create four quadrants.

Loop: Loops are used in coding when something needs to happen more than once. Loops can be used with one piece of code or many. The code inside the loop will run (on repeat) in the order it's placed in,

Origin: The origin is the middle point of a coordinate plane. This is where the X-coordinate and Y-coordinate both equal zero and the two axes cross.

Sequence: Sequence is when something is completed in a specific order. In coding, all programs run in a sequence from top to bottom, meaning the top piece of code will be run first, then the block under it, until the sequence is complete.

Sprite: A sprite is any moveable character or object used in a Scratch project. Sprites can be selected through the Scratch Library, created using drawing tools, or uploaded from the computer.

Variable: A variable is a placeholder for a value and can be made in the Data category of the Scripts tab. The value of a variable can be changed throughout the course of a project. (For example, if a variable was used for the number of lives in a game, you could set it to three at the start of a game. Then each time one sprite touches a certain sprite, the lives variable can be coded to decrease by one.)

Vector mode: The drawing tools in this mode are similar to tools in bitmap mode. However, in vector mode you can create another shape and still go back to a previous one and move it. In this mode, you can also reshape objects that you have made.

X-axis: The X-axis is the axis that runs horizontally (side to side) in a coordinate plane.

Y-axis: The Y-axis is the axis that runs vertically (up and down) in a coordinate plane.

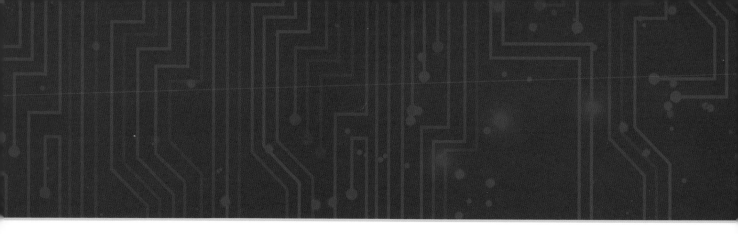

ABOUT THE AUTHOR

Rachel Ziter was raised in Las Vegas, Nevada. She earned a Bachelor of Science in Education and her teaching credentials from Florida Southern College. She has also completed graduate coursework in computer science education at St. Scholastica, as well as professional development in fablab project-based learning at NuVu. Rachel currently works at the Adelson Educational Campus in Las Vegas and is a member of the Tech Team, where she teaches STEM curriculum and instruction, mentors students, and teaches coding and engineering.